Philosophy for children

From child to children

Once upon a time!

We must not deny anything!

Coloring story!

By: Bernardo Octaviano Pereira

This book belongs to:

____

I dedicate this work, firstly, to my parents who I love so much, to my teachers, to my dear aunts and to all my friends, may God bless you all infinitely!

Bernardo Octaviano Pereira

17/04/2024

In a place not far from here, a traveling lady, far from her home and thirsty, knocked on the door of a house looking for a simple glass of water.

However, the owner of the house, known for his stinginess, refused to offer any help, claiming that his well was dry.

The woman, surprised by the denial, insisted that denying water to someone was a merciless action and that Heavenly Father was watching him deny water.

However, his words fell on deaf ears, and she left thirsty, feeling the weight of the man's indifference.

The next morning, when the man went to the well to get water, he was shocked to find that the well was completely dry, depriving him of his most precious source of life.

He realized, too late, that his pettiness had turned against him, leaving him thirsty and helpless.

This bitter experience taught man a valuable lesson: we should not deny others the most precious things we have,

as we may end up needing the same help in the future. Lack of generosity and compassion can leave us empty,

depriving us of the kindness and solidarity we so desperately need in times of need.

Thus, he learned the importance of reaching out to others, sharing the best we have and cultivating a spirit of generosity and empathy.

For ultimately, it is through kindness and compassion that we find true abundance and gratification in our lives.

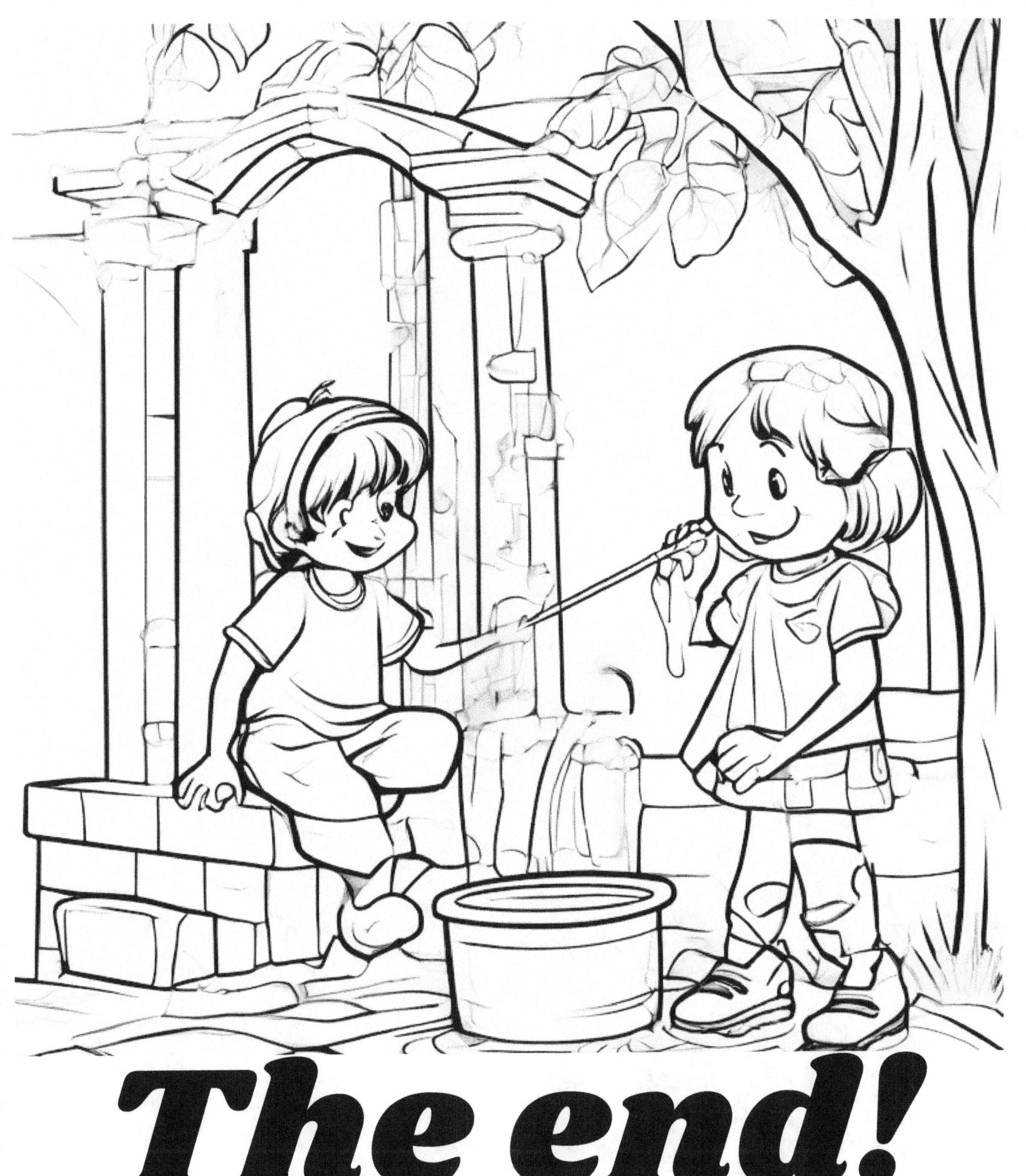

The end!